The Vintage
COLORING
BOOK

The
Vintage
COLORING
BOOK

GORGEOUS VINTAGE DESIGNS TO MAKE YOUR OWN

THUNDER BAY
P·R·E·S·S
San Diego, California

Thunder Bay Press
An imprint of Printers Row Publishing Group
A division of Readerlink Distribution Services, LLC
10350 Barnes Canyon Road, Suite 100, San Diego, CA 92121
www.thunderbaybooks.com

Printers Row Publishing Group is a division of Readerlink Distribution Services, LLC. The Thunder Bay Press name and logo are trademarks of Readerlink Distribution Services, LLC.

All notations of errors or omissions should be addressed to Thunder Bay Press, Editorial Department, at the above address. All other correspondence (author inquiries, permissions) concerning the content of this book should be addressed to Arcturus Holdings Limited, info@arcturuspublishing.com

ISBN: 978-1-62686-472-6
AD004629NT

Printed in China
19 18 17 16 15 4 5 6 7 8

Introduction

Beneficial in so many ways, coloring works as a relaxation technique, calming the mind and occupying the hands. Contrary to popular belief, it unlocks creativity and helps you enter a freer state of being.

This book contains a gorgeous selection of designs, ranging from Victoriana to Art Deco and Pop Art, all ready for you to color in. By taking part in this gentle activity, you can de-stress your mind and body and produce your own beautiful artwork to treasure.

Happy coloring!

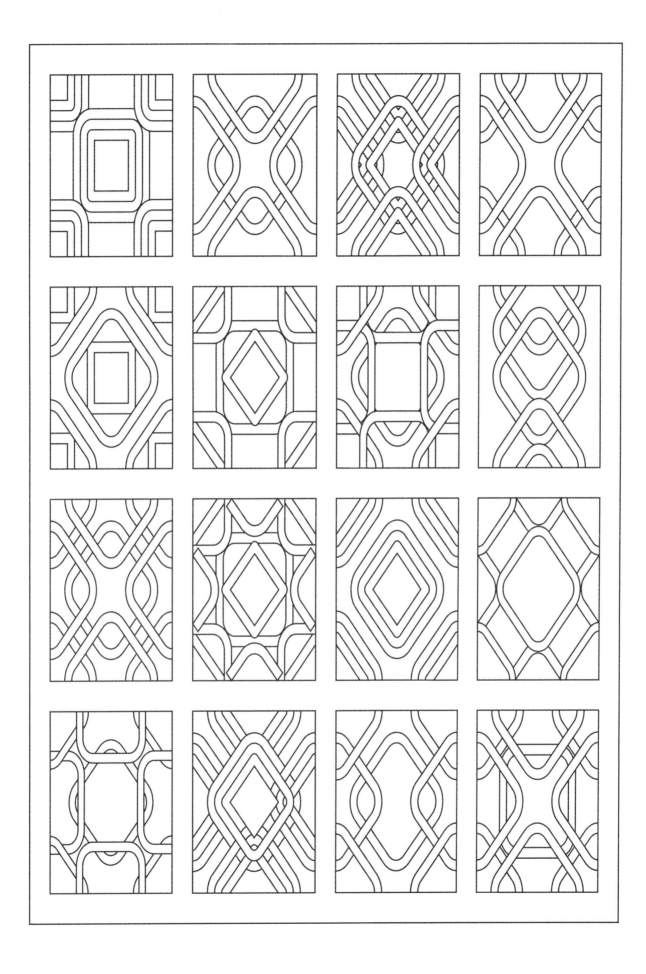

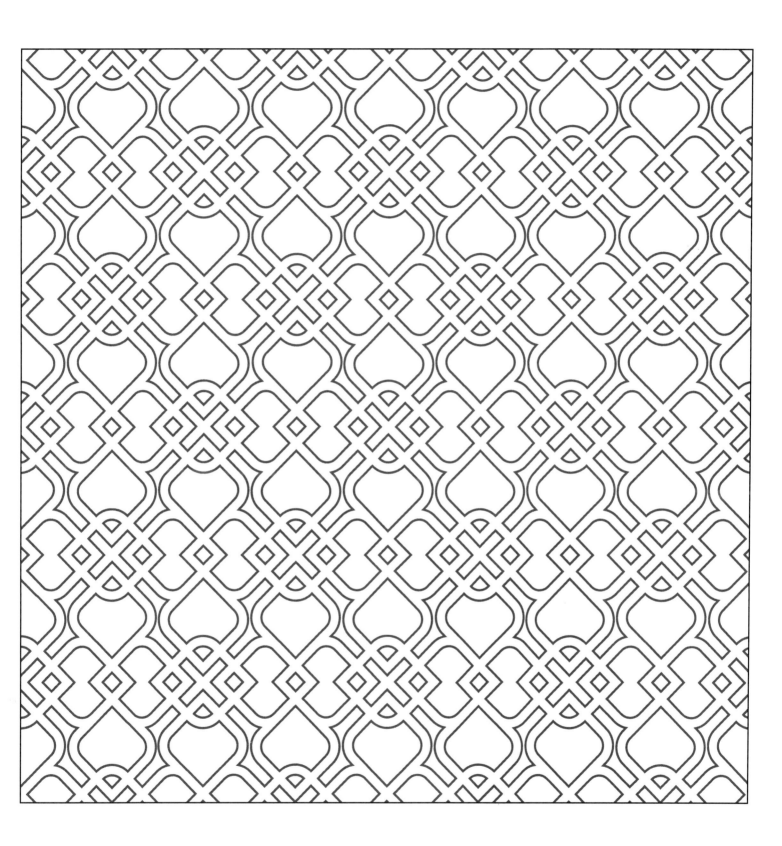

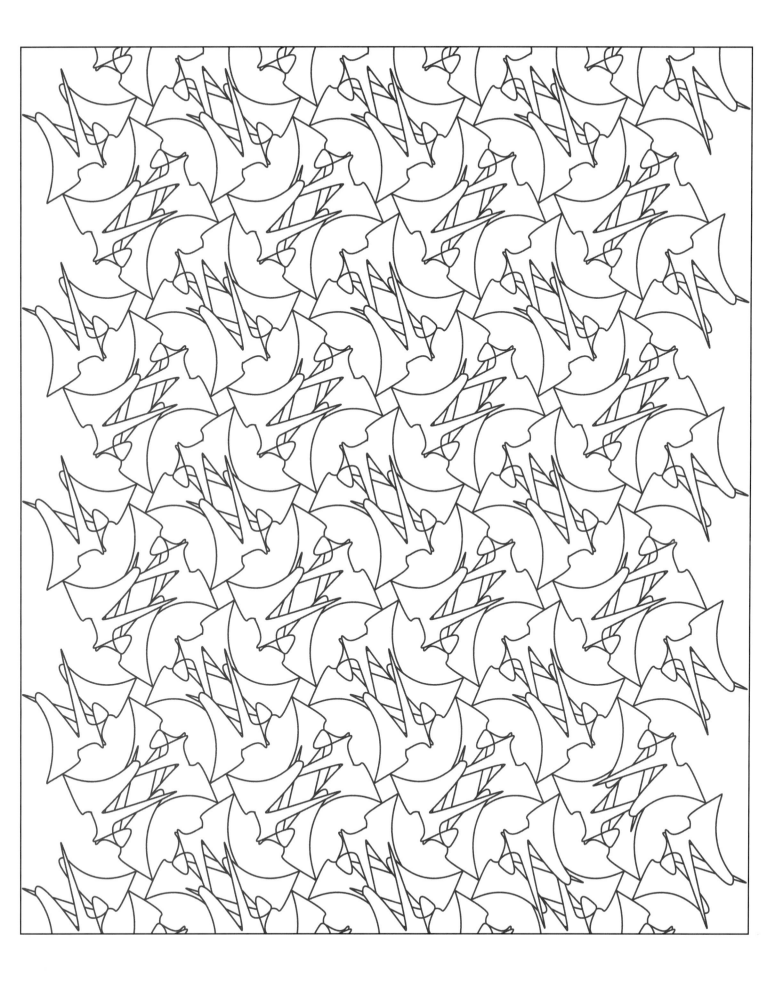

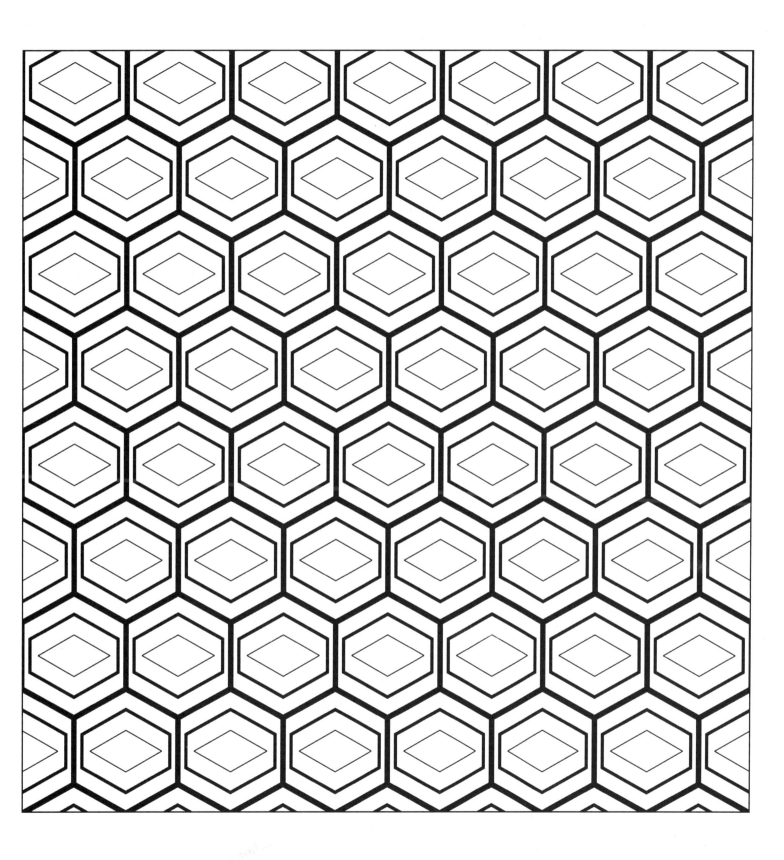